WHY AREN'T YOU SUCCESSFUL? ...YET

THE WORK BOOK

ODUDU 'EMMILLIO' INYANG

WHY AREN'T YOU SUCCESSFUL?... YET
THE WORK BOOK
Copyright © 2022 by Odudu 'Emmillio" Inyang

NAME:

TABLE OF CONTENTS

GROUND 0:
FINDING YOUR NORTH STAR

EXERCISE #00: PRE QUESTIONNAIRE

1. Do you think you are successful? Yes/No (Circle/Highlight your answer)

2. What is success to you? (it's ok to say "I don't know" at this point, what's important is that you can look back at this answer once you have finished the book)

EXERCISE #01: BUCKET LIST

1. Write in bullet points your bucket list. In this list I want you to include the following...

a) All the things you've always wanted to accomplish (e.g. become a millionaire, get married, buy a house, etc)

b) The things you've always wanted to experience (e.g. bungee jumping, riding a jetski)

c) Places you've always wanted to visit (e.g. countries, landmarks, etc)

d) People you've always wanted to meet (e.g. long lost family, celebrities, idols)

e) Other things that you have always wanted to do (e.g. have a heart to heart with someone/trace your family history)

Guide Question:

"You wake up one morning and look at your phone to double check your bank balance to find that you have £1billion in your account. What would your life look like if you had that kind of money?"

ACCOMPLISHMENTS

EXPERIENCES

PLACES

PEOPLE

MISCELLANEOUS

EXERCISE #02: BUCKET LIST QUESTIONNAIRE

Look back at your bucket list and answer the following questions.

1. What emotion(s) would you feel if you achieved the items in your bucket list?

2. What item(s) on your bucket list scare you the most?

3. What item(s) on your bucket list fills you with the most happiness/ fulfilment at the idea of achieving?

4. What item(s) on the bucket list will bring you the most value?

5. What item(s) on the bucket list can you achieve quickly (within 3 months)?

EXERCISE #03: VISION BOARD

- Find at least 1 image for each item of your bucket list and insert it into the box on the next page.
  - ➤ You can achieve this by doing a google image search (or whichever search engine you prefer, or taking a screenshot on your computer/mobile device. If you don't have access to a computer you can try newspapers and/or relevant magazines to your dream (e.g. buying a car magazine that will have pics of the car you want)
- Choose how you want to store them
  - ➤ As a photo album (either on your phone or computer)
  - ➤ As print outs

NB: You don't need to worry about presentation at this point

VISION BOARD

EXERCISE #04: BUCKET LIST MENU

- List the three goals from the previous exercise and research the cost of achieving the goal(s), in as much detail as you can.
  - ➤ E.g. Holiday
    - ▪ Flight
    - ▪ Hotel Accomodation
    - ▪ Travel Money, etc

GOAL 1:

ITEM(S) & COST	TOTAL COST

GOAL 2:

ITEM(S) & COST	TOTAL COST

GOAL 3:

ITEM(S) & COST	TOTAL COST

EXERCISE #05: THE VISION

Write out what your vision is for yourself as if it is a story. Here are some questions to help guide you in your story. **Write this story in the present tense.**

Q1. Who are you? (how do you see yourself, and how do others see you)

Q2. What have you already accomplished?

Q3. What is your life like?

Q4. What do you do during the day/week/month?

Q5. How do you feel?

MY VISION

GROUND 0: HABITUALS

1. Look over bucket list and vision board once a week minimum (5mins)
    a.   Look at what you have already accomplished
    b.   Look at what you haven't...yet
2. Evaluate bucket list and vision board - once a month
    a.   Is this what I still want?
    b.   Is this just as valuable as I saw it last month?

HABITUAL	WEEK 1	WEEK 2	WEEK 3	WEEK 4
BUCKET LIST REMINDER	☐	☐	☐	☐
VISION BOARD REMINDER	☐	☐	☐	☐
BUCKET LIST EVALUATION	☐	☐	☐	☐
VISION BOARD EVALUATION	☐	☐	☐	☐

GROUND 1:
BOOSTING YOUR SELF ESTEEM, SELF CONFIDENCE & CONFIDENCE

EXERCISE #06: PERFECTIONIST QUESTIONNAIRE

Answer the following questions:

Q. Name one example of a situation when you were perfect (If you have one)

Q. If you managed to find one, what was the end result?

Q. Was the end result worth the energy, time and other sacrifices you made?

Q. Think of all the people who you either admire or want to be like. Are any of them perfect?

EXERCISE #07: PERSONAL RIGHTS QUESTIONNAIRE

Please see below a list of personal rights and fill out the following boxes.

NO	I Have The Right	Were you aware this was your right? (Y/N)	How Well do you protect this right? (out of 10)
1	To be safe (physically, mentally, emotionally and spiritually).		
2	To be respected		
3	To be treated fairly.		
4	To have needs & wants.		
5	To listen to my intuition.		
6	To ask for what I feel I need and/or want.		
7	To try.		
8	To make a decision.		
9	To say 'yes'		
10	To say 'no'		
11	To be unsure		
12	To change a decision.		
13	To make a mistake.		
14	To express myself (thoughts, feelings & values)		
15	To forgive myself.		
16	To forgive others.		
17	To express emotion		

NO	I Have The Right	Were you aware this was your right? (Y/N)	How Well do you protect this right? (out of 10)
18	To have a code of honour, or a set of values		
19	To be happy & enjoy life, as I see fit.		
20	To improve and/or try to improve		
21	To be honest		
22	To agree or disagree with someone else		
23	To become the best version of myself, as I see fit"		

EXERCISE #08: PERSONAL BILL OF RIGHTS

Write down your personal bill of rights (If you are not sure, use the list from the previous exercise)

NO	I Have The Right To...
1	
2	
3	
4	
5	
6	
7	
8	
9	
10	
11	
12	
13	
14	
15	
16	
17	
18	
19	
20	

EXERCISE #09: I.P.B. CHART

Come up with at least one Internal Personal Boundary for each of the following categories. Feel free to continue adding to it over time.

➢ Physical - Health	➢ Physical - Space	➢ Mental (Thoughts	➢ Spiritual (Values)
➢ Physical - Time	➢ Physical - Objects/ ➢ Possessions	➢ Emotional (Feelings)	

No	Category	Name of Boundary	Right That It Protects	Exception	Punishment for Violating Boundary	Punishment for not enforcing boundary
1						
2						
3						
4						
5						
6						
7						
8						
9						

No	Category	Name of Boundary	Right That It Protects	Exception	Punishment for Violating Boundary	Punishment for not enforcing boundary
10						
11						
12						
13						
14						
15						
16						
17						
18						

EXERCISE #10: I.P.B. VIOLATION RECORD

In the chart below, note down any and all of your violations to your internal personal boundaries (IPBs)

NB: Charges can include fines or other consequences that you have determined in your IPB chart.

Category

➢ Physical - Health	➢ Physical - Space	➢ Mental (Thoughts	➢ Spiritual (Values)
➢ Physical - Time	➢ Physical – Objects/ Possessions	➢ Emotional (Feelings)	

No	Date	Category	Boundary	Charge	Done?
1					☐
2					☐
3					☐
4					☐
5					☐
6					☐
7					☐
8					☐
9					☐
10					☐
11					☐
12					☐
13					☐
14					☐
15					☐
16					☐
17					☐
18					☐
19					☐
20					☐

Category

➤ Physical - Health	➤ Physical - Space	➤ Mental (Thoughts	➤ Spiritual (Values)
➤ Physical - Time	➤ Physical – Objects/ Possessions	➤ Emotional (Feelings)	

No	Date	Category	Boundary	Charge	Done?
21					☐
22					☐
23					☐
24					☐
25					☐
26					☐
27					☐
28					☐
29					☐
30					☐
31					☐
32					☐
33					☐
34					☐
35					☐
36					☐
37					☐
38					☐
39					☐
40					☐

EXERCISE #11: GOOD ENOUGH LIST

Write a list of people that you consider to be 'good enough' in the following categories. Remember, we are not talking about perfect or excellent, just good enough or better. In these lists, you can include

- People you personally know (e.g. friends/family/colleagues)
- People you don't know (celebrities, heroes,etc)

HEALTH

WEALTH

RELATIONSHIPS

PERSONAL DEVELOPMENT

HAPPINESS

From writing these lists, what have you realised about the people you deem good enough?

How many of these people do you speak to every week?

How many of these people do you speak to every month?

MAKE A POINT TO GET IN TOUCH WITH EVERYONE ON THIS LIST AT LEAST ONCE A MONTH (VIA TEXT, PHONE OR MEET UP). SCHEDULE IT IN YOUR DIARY IF YOU HAVE TO!!!!

EXERCISE #12: R.O.G.E CHART

Write down a list of your qualities that you feel qualifies you to be good enough to accomplish your definition of success. Also give yourself a number out of 10 for each quality
- Write down qualities that you would score yourself a 7/10 minimum on
- Think about the people you have already written down as your definition of good enough and think about the qualities you have in common with them.

NB: There is no quality too small or insignificant to include. The most important thing is to include a quality that you believe to be helpful

NO.	QUALITY	MARK OUT OF 10
1		
2		
3		
4		
5		
6		
7		
8		
9		
10		
11		
12		
13		
14		
15		
16		
17		
18		
19		
20		

EXERCISE #13: [ALREADY DONE] BUCKET LIST

Write down a list of things that you have accomplished/experienced/achieved that you once upon a time had on your bucket list or always wanted to do. Please put at least one in each of the relevant categories

HEALTH

WEALTH/ACCOMPLISHMENTS

RELATIONSHIPS (PEOPLE)

PERSONAL DEVELOPMENT

HAPPINESS (EXPERIENCES)

EXERCISE #14: BRANCH FINDER

List all of the qualities that you believe are necessary to achieve your definition of success.

NB: If you are not sure, run a google/search engine search on the following?
- ➤ **"What are the required qualities to be successful?"**
- ➤ **"What are the required qualities to be happy?"**

NO.	QUALITY	CURRENT MARK OUT OF 10
1		
2		
3		
4		
5		
6		
7		
8		
9		
10		
11		
12		
13		
14		
15		
16		
17		
18		
19		
20		

EXERCISE #15: L.O.G.E. ASSESSMENT

Give yourself a mark out of 10 in the following leaves of good enough (skills). With the use of research, feel free to add others you feel are important

Guide Search Questions?

➢ **"What are the required skills to be successful?"**

➢ **"What are the required skills to be happy?"**

➢ **"What are the required skills to (insert bucket list item or vision for success here)?**

NO.	LEAF	CURRENT MARK OUT OF 10
1		
2		
3		
4		
5		
6		
7		
8		
9		
10		
11		
12		
13		
14		
15		
16		
17		
18		
19		
20		

EXERCISE #16: COMPETENCY QUESTIONNAIRE

1. Pick an item off your bucket list, or name something you'd like to do/achieve.
2. Go to a search engine and search "How to [INSERT YOUR GOAL HERE]"
3. Read at least 3 articles, videos on the subject
4. From your research, what were your five biggest takeaways from it?

GOAL:

Articles

1.

2.

3.

4.

Top 5 Takeaways

1.

2.

3.

4.

5.

Having done this exercise, do you currently see yourself as competent?

How do you feel about the idea of cultivating the competency skills you currently may not have?

GROUND 1: HABITUALS

1. Look over bucket list and vision board once a week minimum (5mins)

    a. Look at what you have already accomplished

    b. Look at what you haven't...yet

2. Evaluate bucket list and vision board - once a month

    a. Is this what I still want?

    b. Is this just as valuable as I saw it last month?

PERSONAL BILL OF RIGHTS REMINDER	WEEK 1	WEEK 2	WEEK 3	WEEK 4
I.P.B CHART REMINDER	☐	☐	☐	☐
GOOD ENOUGH LIST REMINDER	☐	☐	☐	☐
WEEKLY R.O.G.E/ B.O.G.E/ L.O.G.E	☐	☐	☐	☐
PERSONAL BILL OF RIGHTS REMINDER	☐	☐	☐	☐
GRATITUDE JOURNAL	☐☐☐☐☐☐☐	☐☐☐☐☐☐☐	☐☐☐☐☐☐☐	☐☐☐☐☐☐☐

GROUND 2:
CONQUERING YOUR FEARS

EXERCISE #17:'IT' LIST

Write down a list of all the things that you feel that you couldn't handle. In this list include

- Things you have actually experienced and feel like you couldn't handle again
- Things that you haven't experienced, but don't think you could handle
- Things you are scared of (either real or just the thought of)

NB: Feel free to include any and every item from my list that is also relevant to you.

NO	'IT'	Experienced this before? (Y/N)	If Yes, How did you react?
1			
2			
3			
4			
5			
6			
7			
8			
9			
10			
11			
12			
13			
14			
15			
16			
17			
18			
19			

NO	'IT'	Experienced this before? (Y/N)	If Yes, How did you react?
20			
21			
22			
23			

Q. Is there a recurring theme with these Items, and if so, what is it?

The recurring theme is that these fears are based on expectations and assumptions

EXERCISE #18: 'IT' MEDITATION

NB: Read all instructions before starting

❖ Identify at least 5 items from your 'IT' List and write them down.

❖ Do 5x5 (breathing in through your nose for 5 seconds and breathing out through your mouth for 5 seconds)

❖ Spend a total of 5 mins (1min for each item) visualising your IT as if it was currently happening, whilst maintaining your 5x5 breathing

➢ Focus on your five senses in as much details as possible (Sight/Sound/Touch/Feel/Smell)

➢ Imagine breathing in your fear, and then breathing it out, whilst trying to stay as relaxed as possible

❖ Afterwards, in the box provided, write down your thoughts and feelings

NB: Using an interval timer will greatly help you on this, please see below if you have issues finding one

Online Interval Timer
- **https://www.online-stopwatch.com/interval-timer/**

Interval Timer (Chrome Extension)
- **https://chrome.google.com/webstore/detail/interval-timer/glhbffeiigldedfpeiccmfdigplkeanm**

Guide Questions (to be answered after the meditation)

Q. How do you currently feel?

Q. Which items of your 'IT' list did you find most difficult to focus on whilst remaining relaxed?

EXERCISE #19: INTERNAL SENSE
OF SHOULD QUESTIONNAIRE

Write down your expectations that you have in the following categories. Use either of the following statements

I should already be....

I should already have...

NAME:
AGE:

HEALTH

No.	Expectation
1	
2	
3	
4	
5	
6	
7	

WEALTH

No.	Expectation
1	
2	
3	
4	
5	
6	
7	

PERSONAL

No.	Expectation
1	
2	
3	
4	
5	
6	
7	

RELATIONSHIPS

No.	Expectation
1	
2	
3	
4	
5	
6	
7	

HAPPINESS

No.	Expectation
1	
2	
3	
4	
5	
6	
7	

EXERCISE #20: WHY NOT? QUESTIONNAIRE

Identify 5 goals from your bucket list. Under each goal answer the following question.
- Why won't you be able to achieve this?
- What has happened in the past to make you believe this?
- Who has influenced you believing this and what did they say/do to make you believe this?

NB: Write as many reasons and as much detail as you feel necessary. If you are struggling you can simply fill out the questionnaire for Goal 00: My definition of success

GOAL 00: MY DEFINITION OF SUCCESS			
No	Reason Why Not	Past experience that made you feel this	Who influenced you to feel this and how?
1			
2			
3			
4			
5			

GOAL 1:			
No	Reason Why Not	Past experience that made you feel this	Who influenced you to feel this and how?
1			
2			
3			
4			
5			

GOAL 2:			
No	Reason Why Not	Past experience that made you feel this	Who influenced you to feel this and how?
1			
2			
3			
4			
5			

GOAL 3:			
No	Reason Why Not	Past experience that made you feel this	Who influenced you to feel this and how?
1			
2			
3			
4			
5			

GOAL 4:

No	Reason Why Not	Past experience that made you feel this	Who influenced you to feel this and how?
1			
2			
3			
4			
5			

GOAL 5:

No	Reason Why Not	Past experience that made you feel this	Who influenced you to feel this and how?
1			
2			
3			
4			
5			

EXERCISE #21: LIGHT VS DARK CONVO

Write down 5 goals that you want to achieve within the next year (ideally 1 goal from each category of your life that you consider important) and have a conversation with the light and dark versions of yourself in regards to your chances of achieving that goal.

DARK: NEGATIVE (FEAR/PESSIMISM/DOUBT/ANXIETY/ANGER/INSECURITY)
LIGHT: POSITIVE (LOVE/OPTIMISM/CONVICTION/TRUST/CALM/CONFIDENCE)

Goal 1 (Health)
DARK:
LIGHT:
DARK:
LIGHT:
DARK:
LIGHT:
DARK:
LIGHT:
DARK:
LIGHT:
DARK:
LIGHT:
Goal 2 (Wealth)
DARK:
LIGHT:
DARK:
LIGHT:
DARK:
LIGHT:
DARK:
LIGHT:
DARK:
LIGHT:
DARK:
LIGHT:

Goal 3 (Personal Growth)
DARK:
LIGHT:
DARK:
LIGHT:
DARK:
LIGHT:
DARK:
LIGHT:
DARK:
LIGHT:
DARK:
LIGHT:

Goal 4 (Relationships)
DARK:
LIGHT:
DARK:
LIGHT:
DARK:
LIGHT:
DARK:
LIGHT:
DARK:
LIGHT:
DARK:
LIGHT:

Goal 5 (Happiness)
DARK:
LIGHT:
DARK:
LIGHT:
DARK:
LIGHT:
DARK:
LIGHT:
DARK:
LIGHT:
DARK:
LIGHT:

EXERCISE #22: VICTIM STORY

Imagine that none of your problems or the bad in your life is your fault, but the fault of other people. Write down your life story from the perspective of you being the only victim.

Guide Questions
- Who have been and who currently are the villains of your story and held you back from achieving your definition of success/ happiness?
- How have they held you back?
- Why should people feel sorry for you?
- Possible Villains:
    - Another part of you (e.g. past version of yourself)
    - Parents/Family/Friends/Enemies
    - An ex (partner/spouse)

EXERCISE #23: HERO STORY

Imagine that you are now the super hero of your story and have the power to determine how your life turns out. This includes saving the victim, which is the old version of you consumed by fear. Write down your life story from this perspective

Guide Questions
- What's your superpower?
- How do you save your old self?
- What's the origin story of your villains from the previous victim story

What if the villain(s) in your victim story were also victims in their own story?

GROUND 2: HABITUALS

1. Look over bucket list and vision board once a week minimum (5mins)
   a. Look at what you have already accomplished
   b. Look at what you haven't...yet
2. Evaluate bucket list and vision board - once a month
   a. Is this what I still want?
   b. Is this just as valuable as I saw it last month?

HABITUAL	WEEK 1	WEEK 2	WEEK 3	WEEK 4
'IT' LIST	☐	☐	☐	☐
'IT' LIST MEDITATION	☐☐☐☐☐☐☐	☐☐☐☐☐☐☐	☐☐☐☐☐☐☐	☐☐☐☐☐☐☐
LIGHT VS DARK CONVO	☐	☐	☐	☐
VICTIM STORY	☐	☐	☐	☐
HERO STORY	☐	☐	☐	☐

GROUND 3:
LETTING GO & MANIFESTING
THE POWER OF PEOPLE

EXERCISE #24: HURT LIST

Think about all the people who have hurt you in your life and fill in the table below

#	NAME/RELATION	HOW?	EFFECT
1			
2			
3			
4			
5			
6			
7			
8			
9			
10			
11			
12			
13			
14			
15			
16			

#	NAME/RELATION	HOW?	EFFECT
17			
18			
19			
20			
21			
22			
23			
24			
25			
26			
27			
28			
29			
30			
31			
32			
33			
34			

#	NAME/RELATION	HOW?	EFFECT
35			
36			
37			
38			
39			
40			

EXERCISE #25: FORGIVENESS LETTERS

➢ Identify and write a letter of forgiveness to 3 people on your list, who you feel have hurt you the most (if you are struggling, pick 3 people that you feel you are ready to forgive)

➢ Use the information from the previous exercise to answer the following questions
- o What did they do to you?
- o How did it make you feel?
- o Why do you think it made you feel this way?
- o What happened as a result of this? (in the short, medium and long term)
- o What do you think their reason was for doing this? (if you don't know, say so in the letter)

➢ Close each letter with the phrase "I choose to forgive you…

NB: If you don't feel ready to forgive them just yet,

instead of closing out with the forgiveness phrase, answer the following questions instead

➢ **How has this experience already made you a better person?**

➢ **How could this situation(s) make you a better person?**

➢ **What do you feel would need to happen in life for you to forgive them?**

'NB: You can use the template on the next page to write the letter'

LETTER #1

Dear

You hurt me by...

This made me feel...

It made me feel this way because...

What happened as a result was...

If I had to see things from your perspective, I would say I see that...

I choose to forgive you, and the reason why is to better serve myself, also...

I am grateful to you for...

I can and will become a better person from this by...

Sincerely,

LETTER #2

Dear

You hurt me by...

This made me feel...

It made me feel this way because ...

What happened as a result was...

If I had to see things from your perspective, I would say I see that...

I choose to forgive you, and the reason why is to better serve myself, also...

I am grateful to you for…

I can and will become a better person from this by…

Sincerely,

LETTER #3

Dear

You hurt me by...

This made me feel...

It made me feel this way because ...

What happened as a result was...

If I had to see things from your perspective, I would say I see that...

I choose to forgive you, and the reason why is to better serve myself, also ...

I am grateful to you for...

I can and will become a better person from this by...

Sincerely,

EXERCISE #26: VILLAIN LIST

➤ Write down a list of the people in your past and present that you feel may have considered you a villain at some point, or currently see you as a villain.

➤ If you're not sure, think of people that you would consider a villain if what you had done to them had been done to you

#	NAME/RELATION	HOW?	EFFECT
1			
2			
3			
4			
5			
6			
7			
8			
9			
10			
11			
12			
13			
14			

#	NAME/RELATION	HOW?	EFFECT
15			
16			
17			
18			
19			
20			
21			
22			
23			
24			
25			
26			
27			
28			
29			
30			
31			
32			

#	NAME/RELATION	HOW?	EFFECT
33			
34			
35			
36			
37			
38			
39			
40			

EXERCISE #27: APOLOGY LETTER

Using the following template, write a letter to at least one person who you feel you have wronged.

Dear

>

I take full accountability in the fact that I wronged you by...

>

Doing this to you was wrong because...

>

If the shoes were on the other foot, I would have felt...

>

I am truly sorry and ask for your forgiveness. I do however acknowledge that forgiveness is only a choice that you can make.

I am grateful to you for...

I have become, can become and/or will become a better person from this by...

I truly hope you are in a good place and I truly want to wish you to have a great life, whether I am a part of it, or not.

Sincerely,

EXERCISE #28: SELF FORGIVENESS LETTER

Following the template below, write a letter of forgiveness to yourself.

Dear

You hurt me by, and others by...

This made me feel...

It made me feel this way because...

What happened as a result was...

If I had to see things from your perspective, I would say I see that...

What happened as a result was...

I am grateful to you for...

I can and will become a better person from this by...

You don't ever have to feel the need to impress me. You impress me by how you respond, not by what you do. No matter what decisions you make now or in the future. No matter what failure or success you make, I LOVE YOU UNCONDITIONALLY, AND FOREVER WILL.

Sincerely,

EXERCISE #29: 'SELF MADE' STRESS TEST

Answer the questions below, in story form. Include as much detail as possible.

1. What is your proudest achievement?

2. Who helped you? & how?

3. Describe a story of what you have done by yourself?

4. When you think about it, who actually helped you in this achievement you previously felt you had done by yourself?

EXERCISE #30: APPROVAL LIST

Write down a list of the names of people whose approval/disapproval affects you below. Please also add how this affects you.

NB: This can include names, but also categories of people (e.g. colleagues you admire/girlfriends/boyfriends, etc

Whose Approval/Disapproval affects you?

No.	NAME/RELATION	HOW DOES IT AFFECT YOU?
1		
2		
3		
4		
5		
6		
7		
8		
9		
10		

EXERCISE #31: EXTERNAL SENSE
OF SHOULD QUESTIONNAIRE

Fill out the questionnaire below. Once completed, compare your answers for expectations with your answers for assumptions.

EXPECTATIONS
How should people already see me?

No.	Expectation
1	
2	
3	
4	
5	
6	
7	

How should people already treat me?

No.	Expectation
1	
2	
3	
4	
5	
6	
7	

How should people respond when I speak?

No.	Expectation
1	
2	
3	
4	
5	
6	
7	

ASSUMPTIONS
How do I assume people see me?

No.	Assumption
1	
2	
3	
4	
5	
6	
7	

How do I assume people will treat me?

No.	Assumption
1	
2	
3	
4	
5	
6	
7	

How do I assume people respond when I speak?

No.	Assumption
1	
2	
3	
4	
5	
6	
7	

EXERCISE #32: E.P.B. CHART

Come up with at least one External Personal boundary for each of the following categories that apply to you.

NB: Feel free to continue adding to it over time.

Category

➤ Physical - Health	➤ Physical - Space	➤ Mental (Thoughts	➤ Spiritual (Values)
➤ Physical - Time	➤ Physical – Objects/ Possessions	➤ Emotional (Feelings)	

No	Category	Name of Boundary	Exception	Punishment for Violating Boundary	Punishment for not enforcing Boundary
1					
2					
3					
4					
5					
6					
7					
8					
9					
10					
11					
12					
13					
14					
15					
16					
17					
18					
19					
20					

EXERCISE #33: OP-DNW CHART

Write down a list of people you care about and write down what their dreams are. If you don't already know, make a point to ask them

No.	Person - Relationship	What is their dream(s)	What are their needs and wants & How can I help?
1			
2			
3			
4			
5			
6			
7			
8			
9			
10			
11			
12			
13			
14			
15			

No.	Person - Relationship	What is their dream(s)	What are their needs and wants & How can I help?
16			
17			
18			
19			
20			

EXERCISE #34: O.P. QUESTIONNAIRE

Identify at least one goal from your bucket list or any other goal you wish to achieve and fill in the following table as to how you could use each pillar of people to achieve it.

NB: Simply write 'N/A' in any box where you feel like that pillar wouldn't be helpful to achieving your goal.

Goal:

PILLAR	HOW?
Dreams (OPD)	
Needs & Wants (OPNW)	
Time (OPT)	
Energy (OPE)	
Relationships/ Network (OPR)	
Money (OPM)	
Labour (OPL)	
Resources (OPRes)	
Systems (OPS)	
Knowledge (OPK)	
Experiences (OPEx)	
Ideas (OPI)	

EXERCISE #35: HELP LIST

Pick one goal and think about up to 10 people that you feel could help you achieve that goal. In addition, complete the following table:

No.	Person - Relationship	HOW CAN THEY HELP? (Which pillars can they provide and how?)	HOW CAN I HELP THEM IN RETURN? (e.g. Money/Time/ Resources,etc)
1			
2			
3			
4			
5			
6			
7			
8			
9			
10			

EXERCISE #36: HELP JOURNAL

DATE	TASK NEEDING HELP ON	NAME OF HELPER	PREDICTED OUTCOME	WHAT CAN BE DONE TO INCREASE % OF POSITIVE OUTCOME	OUTCOME	REFLECTION (HOW CAN I GROW FROM THIS?

From Completing this exercise, what's your attitude regarding the benefits and drawbacks of receiving help from others?

GROUND 3: HABITUALS

HABITUAL	WEEK 1	WEEK 2	WEEK 3	WEEK 4
HURT LIST (REVIEW)	☐	☐	☐	☐
FORGIVENESS LETTER (1 LETTER)	☐	☐	☐	☐
VILLAIN LIST (REVIEW)	☐	☐	☐	☐
APPROVAL LIST (REVIEW)	☐	☐	☐	☐
E.P.B CHART (REVIEW)	☐	☐	☐	☐

GROUND 4:
ALIGNING YOUR LIFESTYLE WITH YOUR DEFINITION OF SUCCESS

EXERCISE #37: WEEKLY LIFE ASSESSMENT

Using the following ranking system below, mark down each week how you feel about each of the following categories in your life out of 10. For added benefit you can assign 1 goal that you wish to achieve within the next year under each category.

RANKING SYSTEM

SCORE	DESCRIPTION
1	Horrible
2	Really Bad
3	Bad
4	Not Good
5	So-So/Neutral
6	Good
7	Very Good
8	Great
9	Brilliant
10	Amazing

NB: *Continue this exercise every single week to track your progress. The worksheet allows you to do this for 12 months (which is a great sample size to track your progress). Continue doing this whilst reading the rest of the book and beyond.*

Date/ Category	Score (Out of 10)					Notes
	Health	Wealth	Personal Development	Relationships	Happiness	

Date/ Category	Score (Out of 10)					Notes
	Health	Wealth	Personal Development	Relationships	Happiness	

EXERCISE #38: CURRENT LIFESTYLE MAP

Write down your tasks & activities during the next week (with rough durations for important tasks). Also include approximate times you wake up and go to sleep. **NB:** Include what you normally do, rather than what you plan on doing/ Also, if the time you do something varies (e.g. waking up) include the time range of the earliest and latest time you would do it.

	Monday	Tuesday	Wednesday	Thursday	Friday	Saturday	Sunday
Morning: 6am-12pm							
After-Noon: 12pm-5pm							

	Monday	Tuesday	Wednesday	Thursday	Friday	Saturday	Sunday
Evening: 5pm - 11pm							
After Hours/ Early Morn 11pm - 6am							

EXERCISE #39: FUTURE LIFE FORECAST

From going through your current lifestyle map, Answer the following questions.

1. What's your thoughts on your current lifestyle?

2. If you were to live the rest of your life like this (next 50+ years) what would your life be like (within Health/Wealth/Personal Growth/Relationships/Happiness?

3. Based on your current lifestyle map, what would you say your current philosophy/values are? (e.g. instant gratification)

EXERCISE #40: DIET

As truthfully as you can, write down a list of your current diet (what you would consume at least every month). In the following categories & colour code as follows:

Healthy	Moderate: Neither Healthy or Unhealthy	A Little Unhealthy	Completely Unhealthy

No	BREAKFAST (MORNING)	LUNCH (AFTERNOON)	DINNER (EVENING)	SNACKS/ SUPPLEMENTS	DRINKS
1					
2					
3					
4					
5					
6					
7					
8					
9					
10					

If you were to stick to this diet, what do you think your life will look like 10 years into the future?:

What can I do to improve this?:

EXERCISE #41: TERRAIN REPORT

As truthfully as you can, write down your current answers for the following lists, and answer the follow up questions

Colour Code elements of each list by following colours; Green = Adds value, Yellow = Doesn't add or take away value, Orange = Takes away value, Red = Destructive.

ENTERTAINMENT LIST: WHAT YOU WATCH

No	TV (SHOWS/ GENRES)	FILM (GENRES)	ONLINE	SOCIAL MEDIA (E.G. YOUTUBE)	GAMES/OTHER
1					
2					
3					
4					
5					
6					
7					
8					
9					
10					

If you were to stick to this list, what do you think your life will look like 10 years into the future?:

What can I do to improve this?:

READING LIST: WHAT YOU READ

No	BOOKS	WEBSITE/ ARTICLE	NEWSPAPER/MAGAZINE	SOCIAL MEDIA	OTHER
1					
2					
3					
4					
5					
6					
7					
8					
9					
10					

If you were to stick to this list, what do you think your life will look like 10 years into the future?

What can I do to improve this?:

LISTENING LIST: WHAT YOU LISTEN TO

No	MUSIC (GENRES)	PODCASTS	AUDIO BOOKS (GENRES)	GUIDED MEDITATION/ AMBIENCE	OTHER
1					
2					
3					
4					
5					
6					
7					
8					
9					
10					

If you were to stick to this list, what do you think your life will look like 10 years into the future?

What can I do to improve this?:

SOCIAL LIST: WHO YOU SPEND YOUR TIME WITH

No	FAMILY	FRIENDS	COWORKERS	MENTORS	PEERS	CLIENTS/ MENTEES	SIGNIFICANT OTHER
1							
2							
3							
4							
5							
6							
7							
8							
9							
10							
11							
12							
13							
14							
15							

If you were to stick to this list, what do you think your life will look like 10 years into the future?

What can I do to improve this?:

COMMUNITY LIST

No	HEALTH	WEALTH	PERSONAL DEVELOPMENT	RELATIONSHIPS	HAPPINESS
1					
2					
3					
4					
5					
6					
7					
8					
9					
10					

If you were to stick to this list, what do you think your life will look like 10 years into the future?

What can I do to improve this?:

MINDSET - PAST, PRESENT AND FUTURE

What about my past will improve my chances for me to succeed?:

What about my past can make it more difficult for me to succeed?:

How do I feel about my past?:

What is my present mindset?:

How do I feel about my present mindset?:

What do I feel my future will be?:

What emotions do I feel, regarding my future?:

EXERCISE #42: MORNING ROUTINE

Using the chart below (or another one if you prefer), write down the morning routine you want to adopt going forward.

HOUR	TIME	TASK
[1]	00	
	+15	
	+30	
	+45	
[2]	00	
	+15	
	+30	
	+45	

EXERCISE #43: EVENING ROUTINE

Using the chart below (or another one if you prefer), write down the evening routine you want to adopt going forward.

HOUR	TIME	TASK
[1]	00	
	+15	
	+30	
	+45	

EXERCISE #44: LIFESTYLE ATTACHMENT TRADER

Identify up to five unhealthy attachments in your life and lifestyle, then fill out the following sheet with a healthy alternative, and stages to progress from the attachment to the alternative E.g. play games ---(trade with)--- reading a book

UNHEALTHY ATTACHMENT					
↓	↓	↓	↓	↓	
ALTERNATIVE					
STAGE 1					
↓	↓	↓	↓	↓	
STAGE 2					
↓	↓	↓	↓	↓	
STAGE 3					
BENEFIT					
FAIR TRADE? (Y/N)					

EXERCISE #45: TRY JOURNAL

Using the following table, note down any tasks or activities that you already have or are going to try as part of your new lifestyle.

NB: You can especially include in this section all things that you were previously reluctant to try.

NO	DATE	DESCRIPTION (including time of day)	DURATION (if applies) [HR:MINS]	REFLECTION	NEXT STEP
1					
2					
3					
4					
5					
6					
7					
8					
9					
10					
11					
12					
13					
14					
15					
16					

EXERCISE #46: LEVELS OF SELF INTEREST

In the following categories, note down your short term (instantly), medium term (without too much effort) and long term (before retirement age) interests.

NB: The more brutally honest you are, the more you'll get out of this exercise

CATEGORY	HEALTH	WEALTH	RELATIONSHIPS	HAPPINESS	PERSONAL GROWTH
SHORT TERM SELF INTEREST					
MEDIUM TERM SELF INTEREST					
LONG TERM SELF INTEREST					

EXERCISE #47: REWARD LIST

Using the table below, write a list of activities that you would consider a reward

No	REWARD	QUANTITY/DURATION
1		
2		
3		
4		
5		
6		
7		
8		
9		
10		
11		
12		
13		
14		
15		

EXERCISE #48: HAPPINESS LIST

Using the table below, write a list of activities that make you happy, including how often and for how long you would need to do it to make you happy

NB: Add items across all categories (Health, Wealth, Relationships, Happiness, Personal Growth.

No	CATEGORY	DESCRIPTION	FREQUENCY	DURATION
1				
2				
3				
4				
5				
6				
7				
8				
9				
10				
11				
12				
13				
14				
15				

EXERCISE #49: LIFESTYLE 2.0

Using the worksheet below, detail your new. Lifestyle in similar fashion to how you detailed the lifestyle map

Examples of things to also schedule: Morning Routine/Evening Routine/ Habituals/Items from Happiness List

	Monday	Tuesday	Wednesday	Thursday	Friday	Saturday	Sunday
Morning: 6am-12pm							
After-Noon: 12pm - 5pm							

	Monday	Tuesday	Wednesday	Thursday	Friday	Saturday	Sunday
Evening: 5pm - 11pm							
After Hours/ Early Morn 11pm- 6am							

GROUND 4: HABITUALS

HABITUAL	WEEK 1	WEEK 2	WEEK 3	WEEK 4
WEEKLY LIFE ASSESSMENT	☐	☐	☐	☐
DIET	☐	☐	☐	☐
TERRAIN REPORT				☐
MORNING & EVENING ROUTINE (REVIEW)	☐			
TRY JOURNAL	☐	☐	☐	☐
REWARD & HAPPINESS LIST (REVIEW)		☐		
LIFESTYLE 2.0				☐

EXERCISE #50: POST QUESTIONNAIRE

Do you think you are successful? Yes/No (Circle/Highlight your answer)

What is success to you?

How does this compare to your answer at the beginning of this journey? (pre-questionnaire)

YOU MADE IT!!!!!!
WELL DONE & BEST OF LUCK
WITH THE NEW CHAPTER IN YOUR LIFE

Printed in Great Britain
by Amazon

79994189R00072